The Magimix is one of the most time and labour-saving pieces of mo kitchen equipment and the Microwave oven is another. With both you can c fastest cooking in the world. Each in its own special way eases and speec cooking process, taking all the drudgery out of preparation. Both are eff clean and easy to use, eliminating risk of cuts and burns. But neither machi achieve the ultimate in well-cooked appetizing food without *you* the cook, because machines can't shop and plan for you, select ingredients, choose the correct thickness of slices or determine exactly when the food is cooked to perfection. I love cooking and find it challenging and therapeutic and this interest has been stimulated by my Magimix and my Microwave. Now I can concentrate all my energy and imagination on the creative aspects of cooking. There is no more tedious chopping, no more daunting stacks of dirty pots and pans.

The Magimix with its variety of blades and discs will chop, slice, grate and mix to perfection provided you do not overwork the ingredients. Similar attention needs to be paid to Microwave cookery, for with its speed care must be taken *not* to overcook.

You will find all basic intructions in the guide book that comes with any appliance and I include these in my Microwave cookbooks. You will know the rules of stirring and turning. Microwave ovens vary, some have turntables and some don't because their manufacturers claim that with ultra efficient wave distribution, turning is unnecessary. However on older models you may like to turn dishes to ensure even results. It is best to do this 3 times during the cooking period in a 90° arc and always in the same direction. When foods being cooked covered require stirring, you may find it better to use a lid or greaseproof paper. Cling film, put on loosely seals in all the heat and makes for speedier cooking, but it is not practical to reposition it each time that stirring is required. To overcome this give the sealed dish a gentle shake while holding it with oven gloves. Take care when peeling back the cling film not to scald your fingers as there will be some escape of hot steam. Cooking dishes, casseroles and containers must be microwave proof. These include most ceramics, china, heatproof glass, paper and some plastics. Metal or

Contents

metal trim are unsuitable and your guidebook explains this. Although microwave cooking is always simple, preparation by Magimix ensures even more successful results.

Magimix sliced vegetables are uniform in thickness which hand slicing cannot achieve. It guarantees a more even texture and eliminates the chance of finding a harder piece here and there. Grated or finely chopped onions develop a better flavour and it goes without saying that soups puréed in the Magimix save the onerous chore of pushing through a sieve with a wooden spoon.

Meat requiring long slow cooking may be cooked in the microwave oven, set on low or defrost. For speedy results cooked at High power, use 'frying cuts' or tenderize the meat. Chopping is an efficient method to do this and is economical because cheaper cuts can be used. Using the double-bladed knife chop as coarsely or finely as you wish.

Fish is succulent when cooked by microwave. Chop or pound the flesh in the Magimix for fish balls and the more sophisticated quenelles.

As microwave cooks so fast herbs do not get a chance to infuse. If these are chopped in the Magimix even distribution results in a better flavour.

Microwave dishes benefit from attractive garnishing – so use the food processor to chop roasted nuts, grate browned breadcrumbs, stale cake and sweet biscuits or cheese for sweet or savoury toppings. Use the ripple or julienne discs for shaped garnishes and matchsticks of carrots, turnips etc.

Quick cakes and puddings can be prepared on demand and a sauce to go with them is no bother at all.

Use the slicing disc for quick jams and marmalades and the fruit press for juicing. There is not enough space here to list all the tasks it can do in relation to microwave cookery.

High settings (625-650 watts) have been used throughout, suitable for all models but if yours is less than 600 watts, allow a slightly longer cooking time. The latent heat will allow cooking to continue after the oven is switched off, so do not overcook but leave to stand, covered. This will keep the dish happily warm for a few minutes until you are ready to serve.

Because these recipes are so easy to prepare you may get carried away and cook several batches. You can freeze nearly all the dishes, except those including mayonnaise or soured cream. Thaw gently in the microwave oven either continuously on the defrost setting, or at high, switching on intermittently for a few seconds followed by a standing time.

I hope the recipes in this booklet show that the Magimix and Microwave go hand in hand to produce quick dishes that are exciting, attractive and delicious. All are easy to prepare and no one will ever guess that you haven't spent hours slaving over the proverbial hot stove.

Cecilia Norman

The Microwave Cooking School
Hampstead, N.W.3.

Cover photograph shows: Sweet & Sour Pork Meatballs, Chocolate Orange Pyramids, Curried Chicken Suprêmes Mayonnaise, Cream of Watercress Soup, Clear Citrus Marmalade, Rhubarb & Apple Conserve, Spicy Bran Ring.

Soups and Starters

Cream of Watercress Soup

Your guests will think you have spent ages preparing this rich-tasting pale creamy soup. Serve from the tureen or in individual dishes, garnished with a few watercress leaves.

Cut away the stalks, rinse and dry the watercress.

Use the double-bladed knife: Process the watercress for 1 minute. While the motor is still running add the stock, flour and butter. Pour into a large bowl or tureen. Stir in the milk and season to taste with salt and pepper. MICROWAVE ON HIGH for 8 to 10 minutes, stirring two or three times. Add extra stock or milk if necessary.

Reheat and stir in the cream just before serving. Garnish with watercress leaves.

APPROX TIME 10 MINUTES

Serves 3 to 4

1½ bunches watercress
300ml (½ pt) chicken stock
25g (1 oz) flour
40g (1½ oz) butter
450ml (¾ pt) milk
Salt, pepper
3 tbsp single cream
Few watercress leaves to garnish

Potage Crécy

A textured yellow/orange coloured soup with an imperceptibly sweet nuance. Although stock cubes could be substituted the flavour will not match that of real home-made stock.

Use the slicing disc: Process all but one of the carrots, the leek, celery and parsley. Put into a large bowl or tureen with 600ml (1 pt) of the stock and the bay leaves. Partially cover and MICROWAVE ON HIGH for 15 minutes or until the vegetables are very soft. Remove the bay leaves.

Use the double-bladed knife: Process the mixture finely adding the lemon peel. (You may need to do this in two batches.) Pour into the tureen. Add the remaining stock, cream and butter and season well with salt and pepper.

Use the julienne disc: Shred the remaining carrot. Mix with the milk and sugar in a medium bowl and MICROWAVE ON HIGH for 5 minutes, stirring occasionally.

Reheat the soup by MICROWAVING ON HIGH for 2 or 3 minutes, stir occasionally and do not allow to boil. Stir in the carrot mixture and sprinkle with chopped parsley.

APPROX TIME 18 MINUTES

Serves 6 to 8

450g (1 lb) fresh carrots, peeled
1 small leek, trimmed & washed
3 celery stalks
Few sprigs of parsley
1l (1½ pt) hot home-made chicken stock
2 bay leaves
2.5cm (1") piece thinly pared lemon rind
150ml (¼ pt) double cream
20g (¾ oz) butter
Salt, pepper
3 tbsp milk
¼ tsp sugar
2 tsp chopped parsley to garnish

Soupe Piperade

APPROX TIME 13½ MINUTES

Serves 6 to 8

1 small lemon
1 large green pepper, cored & deseeded
1 red pepper, cored & deseeded
1 clove garlic, peeled
1 small onion
25g (1 oz) butter
25g (1 oz) flour
750ml (1¼ pt) chicken stock
150ml (¼ pt) milk
Salt, pepper

A soup to be eaten cold on a warm summer's day but may be gently reheated in the microwave oven if preferred. The smooth orange coloured purée is flecked with red and green.

Halve the lemon lengthwise and remove a sliver from either end so that the lemon will balance.

Use the thick slicing disc: Slice the lemon and set aside for garnish. Slice the green and red peppers, garlic and onion together.

Put the butter in a large bowl or tureen and MICROWAVE ON HIGH for 30 seconds until melted. Stir in the flour and the sliced vegetables and MICROWAVE ON HIGH for 5 minutes until softened, stirring from time to time. Add ½ pint of the stock, part cover and MICROWAVE ON HIGH for 6½ to 7 minutes until the vegetables are very soft.

Use the double-bladed knife: Process the soup in the Magimix bowl until puréed. Combine in the tureen with the remaining stock and milk, adding salt and pepper to taste. Chill for several hours.

Float lemon slices on top just before serving.

Chinese Potato and Sweet Corn Soup

APPROX TIME 17 MINUTES

Serves 6 to 8

2 medium leeks, trimmed & washed
1 clove garlic, crushed
15g (½ oz) butter
900ml (1½ pt) chicken stock
2 bay leaves
225g (8 oz) potato, peeled & quartered
198g (7 oz) can sweetcorn kernels
Salt, pepper

No monosodium glutamate or artificial flavourings are used in this thick soup. It is a delicious green colour spattered with golden sweet corn. The soup is best kept for at least 12 hours for the flavours to develop before reheating.

Use the slicing disc: Slice the leeks. Put the leeks and garlic in a bowl or tureen with the butter and MICROWAVE ON HIGH for 3 minutes, stirring occasionally. Add half the stock and the bay leaves. Partially cover and MICROWAVE ON HIGH for 5 minutes, stirring once.

Use the julienne cutter or coarse grater: Shred the potatoes. Add the potatoes, sweetcorn and remaining stock to the leeks. Partially cover and MICROWAVE ON HIGH for 10 minutes, stirring occasionally until the potato is cooked and the soup thickened. Remove the bay leaves and season to taste with salt and pepper.

Prawn Savoury Cheesecake

A luxury centrepiece to set dinner party conversation off to a good start. The cake freezes well and although best thawed out at room temperature this can be speeded up in the Microwave Oven set on low for a minute or two. If you are using prawns still in their frozen state, chop these separately using the double-bladed knife and fold into the blended cheese a few at a time.

Put the butter in a small bowl and MICROWAVE ON HIGH for 1 to 1½ minutes until melted.

Use the double-bladed knife: Process the biscuits to fine crumbs. Add the butter, lemon rind, salt and pepper and process to a smooth paste. Scrape out the mixture from the Magimix bowl and press into the base of a 23cm (9") loose bottomed flan tin. Chill while preparing the filling.

Use the double-bladed knife: Without washing the Magimix bowl process the cottage cheese until smooth. Add the cream cheese, tomato ketchup and process until well blended.

Put the water in a small jug and MICROWAVE ON HIGH for 20 seconds until the water boils. Sprinkle on the gelatine and stir thoroughly until dissolved. Mix in the lemon juice and continue stirring until the mixture clears.

Start the motor running and pour the dissolved gelatine into the cheese mixture. Then add the prawns so that they are roughly chopped.

Pour the mixture into the prepared flan tin and smooth the surface with a warmed knife.

Refrigerate until set and decorate with lemon twists, cucumber slices and whole prawns.

APPROX TIME 10 MINUTES
+ SETTING TIME

Serves 6 to 8

75g (3 oz) butter
175g (6 oz) cream crackers
2 level tsp grated lemon rind
¼ tsp salt
¼ tsp freshly ground black pepper
225g (8 oz) cottage cheese
225g (8 oz) cream cheese
4 tbsp tomato ketchup
3 tbsp water
1 level tbsp powdered gelatine
2 tbsp lemon juice
225g (8 oz) shelled prawns
Lemon slices, slit & twisted
Cucumber slices
4 to 6 large unshelled cooked prawns

Farmhouse Pâté

APPROX TIME 9 MINUTES
Serves 4
1 medium onion
1 clove garlic
50g (2 oz) unsalted butter
100g (4 oz) chicken livers
100g (4 oz) trimmed pork
4 rashers streaky bacon, de-rinded & boned
1 tsp chopped fresh or frozen sage
2 tbsp brandy
2 tbsp double cream
Salt
Freshly ground black pepper
1 bay leaf

This is a nice coarse pâté that is not too fatty. Double the quantity if you like and cook for just under double the minimum time given.

Use the double-bladed knife: Finely chop the onions and garlic. Put in a shallow dish with half the butter.

MICROWAVE ON HIGH for 2½ to 3½ minutes, stirring occasionally until the onion is soft and just coloured.

Use the double-bladed knife: Chop the livers, pork and bacon. Stir into the sautéed onions with the sage. Cover with greaseproof paper and MICROWAVE ON HIGH for 4 to 5 minutes or until the meat is cooked, stirring occasionally.

Use the double-bladed knife: Process the pâté until smooth, adding the brandy and cream while the motor is running. Season to taste with salt and pepper.

Put the remaining butter in a small bowl and MICROWAVE ON HIGH for ½ to 1 minute until melted and transparent.

Spoon the pâté into a dish (the individual oval brown pottery Divertimenti dishes are very attractive). Pour over the butter and decorate with a bay leaf.

Meat and Poultry

Beef and Mushroom Stroganoff

APPROX TIME 15 MINUTES
Serves 3 to 4
225g (8 oz) button mushrooms
1 small onion
350g (¾ lb) frying steak, trimmed
1 tbsp vegetable oil
1 rounded tbsp flour
¼ level tsp salt
¼ level tsp black pepper
⅛ tsp bayleaf powder
150ml (¼ pt) white wine
4 tbsp double cream

Use the browning dish to seal and brown the meat, although you will still be able to cook the recipe in an ordinary dish, which must not be pre-heated.

Heat the empty browning dish in the MICROWAVE ON HIGH for 5 minutes while preparing the ingredients.

Use the slicing disc: Process the mushrooms and remove from the Magimix bowl.

Use the double-bladed knife: Chop the onion and remove from the Magimix bowl, then process the beef a few lumps at a time, switching on the motor briefly. Remove each batch once it is roughly chopped.

Without removing the browning dish from the microwave oven put in the oil and stir in the onions. This should be done as rapidly as possible. MICROWAVE ON HIGH for 1 minute. Add the meat, MICROWAVE ON HIGH for 2 minutes, then toss quickly and MICROWAVE ON HIGH for a further 2 minutes. Stir in the flour, salt, pepper and bay leaf powder, then the wine and mushrooms. Cover with the lid and MICROWAVE ON HIGH for 5 to 6 minutes, stirring occasionally. Mix in the cream and without covering MICROWAVE ON HIGH for 15 seconds to reheat.

Serve with pre-cooked rice.

To cook rice in the microwave oven – put rice, salt and plenty of boiling water in a deep dish. Without covering MICROWAVE ON HIGH for 10 to 15 minutes until the rice is cooked. Drain in a colander and put under cold running water to separate the grains. Leave to drain thoroughly. To reheat: MICROWAVE ON HIGH for 1 to 2 minutes.

Curried Chicken Suprêmes Mayonnaise

APPROX TIME 11 MINUTES
+ COOLING TIME

Serves 4 to 6

Makes 450ml (¾ pt) mayonnaise

4 to 6 chicken breasts, skinned
Salt, pepper
2 egg yolks
Good pinch mustard
300ml (½ pt) salad oil
2 tbsp fresh lemon juice
1 to 2 level tsp curry powder or to taste
3 to 4 tbsp single cream
¼ iceberg lettuce
¼ cucumber, washed
8 slices tomato

First cook the chicken and leave until cold before coating with the mayonnaise. A boned chicken breast takes just on 2 minutes to cook. Allow 6 to 8 minutes per pound.

To cook, season the chicken with salt and pepper. Place in a single layer in a large shallow dish and cover with greaseproof paper. MICROWAVE ON HIGH for 3 to 4 minutes, then turn the pieces over, moving the end pieces to the middle. Cover again and MICROWAVE ON HIGH for 3 to 4 minutes until the chicken is just cooked and no longer pink inside. Leave for a few minutes, then cool rapidly.

Make the mayonnaise in the Magimix.

Use the double-bladed knife: Start the motor and drop the egg yolks through the feed tube. Add the mustard, salt and pepper. As soon as the mixture foams, pour in the oil in a slow steady stream, processing until the mayonnaise thickens. Add the lemon juice and then the remaining oil with the motor still running. Add the curry powder, switching on and off briefly, then thin down with cream to a coating consistency.

Transfer the chicken to a wire rack over a tray and carefully spoon some mayonnaise over each piece..

Use the slicing disc: Process the lettuce and cucumber and spread on a chilled serving dish. Arrange the chicken pieces on top and garnish with tomato slices.

Beef Casserole with Red Wine

APPROX TIME 22 MINUTES
Serves 3 to 4
450g (1 lb) lean buttock steak
2 medium onions
25g (1 oz) flour
4 tbsp vegetable oil
6 tbsp hot water
150ml (¼ pt) red wine
396g (14 oz) can tomatoes
1 beef stock cube
1 bay leaf
225g (8 oz) sliced vegetables, (optional)
Salt, pepper
1 rounded tsp sweet paprika

A basic casserole in a tasty wine sauce. Add finely sliced carrots, mushrooms, celery or green beans as you wish, allowing a few more minutes cooking time.

Trim the beef and cut into large chunks.

Use the double-bladed knife: Add the meat and process until jagged and roughly chopped but not minced.

Use the double-bladed knife: Finely chop the onions.

Mix the flour and oil together in a large shallow dish and MICROWAVE ON HIGH for 3 to 5 minutes or until light brown and sizzling. Quickly stir in the meat and onion and MICROWAVE ON HIGH for 10 minutes, stirring once during cooking.

Stir in the water, wine, tomatoes and juice, crumbled stock cube, bay leaf and any vegetables of your choice. Season to taste with salt, pepper. Stir in the paprika.

Cover and MICROWAVE ON HIGH for 15 to 18 minutes, stirring occasionally until microwave tender.

Liver and Bacon Casserole

APPROX TIME 19 MINUTES
Serves 4
450g (1 lb) lambs' liver
Flour, well seasoned with salt, pepper and garlic powder
150g (5 oz) (5 slices) bread
1 level tsp dried thyme
3 or 4 sprigs parsley, stalks removed
2 medium onions
5 rashers streaky bacon
Approx 300ml (½ pt) beef stock

Serve this casserole with green beans and Vichy carrots (see page 22)

Slice the liver and toss in the seasoned flour. Put into a deep dish.

Use the double-bladed knife: Remove the crusts and tear the bread roughly, then process into crumbs. Remove from the Magimix bowl. Process the herbs, parsley and onions until finely chopped. Add the breadcrumbs and switch on briefly to mix lightly. Spread the mixture over the liver.

Remove the rind and lay the bacon slices on a plate. Cover with kitchen paper. MICROWAVE ON HIGH for 2½ to 3½ minutes until crisp. Cut the rashers in half.

Use the double-bladed knife: Roughly chop the bacon. Spread the chopped bacon over the crumbs.

Pour over sufficient stock to just cover the crumbs. Cover with greaseproof paper and MICROWAVE ON HIGH for 13 to 18 minutes or until the liver is cooked, turning the dish 90° three or four times during cooking if necessary.

Sweet and Sour Pork Meat Balls

This is a tasty way of using up left-over meat. You could substitute beef, lamb or chicken. The rice softens the mixture but use bread instead if you wish.

Use the double-bladed knife: Cut the meat into manageable pieces and process until finely chopped. Reserve two pineapple rings and the juice. Add the remaining pineapple, the egg, ginger, salt and pepper to the Magimix bowl and process until mixed with the meat to a soft consistency. Remove the blade and stir in the rice.

Form the mixture into 12 balls and arrange in a large shallow dish. MICROWAVE ON HIGH for 3 minutes, then reposition the balls.

Use the double-bladed knife: While the meat is cooking, process all the sauce ingredients together including the reserved juice.

Pour the sauce over the meat and MICROWAVE ON HIGH for 3 minutes, turning the balls over half way through the cooking time.

Garnish with the remaining pineapple rings cut into quarters.

APPROX TIME 8 MINUTES

Serves 4

350g (12 oz) cooked pork
234g (8¼ oz) can pineapple rings
1 egg
¼ tsp ground ginger
½ tsp salt
¼ tsp pepper
2 rounded tbsp cooked long grain rice

4 tbsp wine vinegar
2 tsp vegetable oil
2 tsp soy sauce
¼ tsp black pepper
40g (1½ oz) dark brown sugar
1 level tsp cornflour

Fish and Shellfish

Trout Florentine

This is a way of serving trout without hurting the feelings of sensitive guests. Thaw frozen trout before cooking.

Remove the heads, gut and rinse the trout and dip in seasoned flour.

Put half the butter in a dish large enough to fit in 4 trout in a single layer. MICROWAVE ON HIGH for 1 minute or until melted.

Lay the trout in the dish and baste with the melted butter. Pour over the wine. Cover with greaseproof paper and MICROWAVE ON HIGH for 5 minutes. Turn the fish changing places 'sides to middle' MICROWAVE ON HIGH for 3 to 4 minutes or until cooked and flaky. Lift carefully on to a wooden board and using a table knife slit down the back and ease out the bone. Remove the skin and return the fish to the dish, cover and leave while preparing the vegetables.

Use the double-bladed knife: Separately process the onion, the mushrooms and the spinach with the herbs.

Put the remaining 40g (1 ½ oz) butter in a large bowl, add the onion and MICROWAVE ON HIGH for 2 minutes. Stir in the mushrooms and MICROWAVE ON HIGH for a further 2 minutes. Add the spinach, thyme, grated lemon rind and a shake of salt and pepper. Cover and MICROWAVE ON HIGH for 4 minutes or until the spinach is cooked.

Using a slotted spoon transfer the mixture to a warm serving dish.

To reheat the fish cover and MICROWAVE ON HIGH for 2 to 3 minutes. Remove the two outer fish and arrange on the spinach while MICROWAVING the remaining fish for a further ½ to 1 minute so that they are equally heated through.

Garnish with lemon slices and parsley or thyme sprigs.

APPROX TIME 23 MINUTES

Serves 4

4 medium sized trout
Flour, seasoned with salt & pepper
75g (3 oz) butter
4 tbsp white wine
1 small onion
175g (6 oz) mushrooms
450g (1 lb) fresh spinach, stems removed & torn roughly
2 level tsp fresh or frozen lemon thyme leaves
2 level tsp grated lemon rind
Salt, pepper
Lemon slices
Parsley or thyme sprigs

Halibut for a Summer's Evening

APPROX TIME 11 MINUTES
Serves 4
300g (12 oz) button mushrooms, wiped
15g (½ oz) butter
450g (1 lb) fresh halibut fillet, skinned & cut into 4 even pieces
Salt, pepper
½ clove garlic
½ slender cucumber
1 rounded tsp dried dill weed
For Soured Cream:
150ml (¼ pint) single cream
Juice ½ lemon
(stirred together, then left for ½ hour to thicken)

Prepare the dish a few hours ahead and keep in the refrigerator so that it is cold and fresh to the palate. Double the quantity if you wish. It saves time if you sour the cream first.

Use the slicing disc: Process the mushrooms and put into a shallow dish. Dot with the butter and cover. MICROWAVE ON HIGH for 3 minutes, stirring occasionally. Tip the dish and spoon away the surplus juices.

Season the fish with salt and pepper and rub the flesh with the cut garlic clove which you then discard. Arrange the fish on the mushrooms and sprinkle the surface with dill weed. Cover and MICROWAVE ON HIGH for 4 minutes. Reposition the fish so that the outside pieces are transferred to the middle. MICROWAVE ON HIGH for 2-3 minutes until the fish is cooked.

Leave to cool in the dish or transfer to a serving platter with a slotted spoon.

Use the slicing disc: Without peeling process the cucumber keeping it upright throughout to maintain even shaped slices. Arrange the cucumber slices over and around the sides of the fish. Coat thickly with the homemade soured cream.

Quenelles

APPROX TIME 12 MINUTES
Serves 4
¾kg (1¼ lb) fresh haddock fillet skinned
1 bay leaf
small piece of onion
3-4 tbsp milk
2 large egg whites
4 slices bread, crusts removed

Use the fish skins to make stock. Put them in a large bowl, just cover with water and add salt, pepper and a tiny piece of onion with a bay leaf. MICROWAVE ON HIGH for 8 to 10 minutes until the skins are soft and the liquid cloudy. Strain. The stock will form a jelly when cold and can be stored for a day or two in the refrigerator.

In this recipe milk can be substituted but the flavour will be affected.

Use the double-bladed knife: Process the fish, milk, egg whites and bread torn into pieces. Add the cream and stock, salt, pepper and nutmeg and process briefly. The mixture should be softer than you would expect for ordinary fish balls.

Empty the soup into a large shallow dish and add the water. MICROWAVE ON HIGH for 3 minutes, then stir to blend evenly.

Using two tablespoons shape about 12 oval quenelles and gently put them into the soup, making sure that they are well spaced out.

Without covering, MICROWAVE ON HIGH for 5 to 6 minutes, repositioning the fish twice during cooking until the quenelles cut easily and are white throughout. Cover tightly and leave for 5 minutes before serving or refrigerate for 12 to 24 hours and serve cold.

2 to 3 tbsp thick double cream
6 tbsp fish stock *or* milk
1 level tsp salt
¼ level tsp pepper
¼ level tsp grated nutmeg
298g (10½ oz) can condensed cream of celery soup
300ml (½ pt) hot boiled water

Pacific Bay Shrimp and Oyster à la King

APPROX TIME 12 MINUTES
Serves 6 to 8
150g (5 oz) cream crackers
25g (1 oz) soft margarine
15g (½ oz) flour
300ml (½ pt) milk
2 large eggs
150ml (¼ pt) double cream
Salt, pepper
12 oysters
400g (14 oz) peeled shrimps
25g (1 oz) stale Cheddar cheese, grated

This is an extravagant luxury dish to serve as a starter or light main course with pasta or rice. Fresh oysters are obtainable from fishmongers, but you can use the frozen or bottled variety available at speciality grocers.

Use the double-bladed knife: Process the biscuits until coarsely crushed.

Use the double-bladed knife: Process the margarine and flour together. Leave in the Magimix bowl.

Put the milk in a large jug. MICROWAVE ON HIGH for 2 minutes or until nearly boiling.

Use the double-bladed knife: Switch on the motor and pour the milk, followed by the eggs through the feed tube. Mix in the cream and pour the mixture back into the jug. MICROWAVE ON HIGH for 1 minute until the mixture thickens slightly. Season sparingly with salt and pepper.

Spread a third of the crumbs in a greased shallow dish and arrange the oysters on top. Sprinkle with a layer of crumbs, cover with the shrimps, then the remaining crumbs and pour the sauce over the top.

MICROWAVE ON HIGH for 6 to 7 minutes until the sauce is light and spongy, turning the dish 90° three times during cooking if necessary.

Cover and leave to stand for 5 minutes, then sprinkle with cheese and brown lightly under the grill.

Vegetables and Vegetarian

Vegetarian Roof Top Omelette

APPROX TIME 2½ MINUTES
Serves 1
1 large egg
4 button mushrooms
¼ green pepper
1 tomato
Salt, pepper

Here is a filling yet low calorie supper dish or vegetable accompaniment to a beef sauté that may be multiplied as many times as you like. There is appreciably little difference in the time factor between one or four servings.

For each serving beat one large egg and pour into a greased individual cereal bowl.

Use the slicing disc: Process the mushrooms, pepper and tomato. Remove the disc and season with salt and pepper while still in the Magimix bowl. Spoon the vegetables on top of the egg and MICROWAVE ON HIGH for 2½ to 3 minutes (3 bowls at the same time will take 5 to 5½ minutes). Turn the bowls if necessary once during cooking. Turn out on to dinner plates and serve at once, with a chunk of French bread and butter.

Bavarian Red Cabbage

APPROX TIME 15 MINUTES
+ STANDING TIME
Serves 8
½ red cabbage
1 x 225g (8 oz) cooking apple
2 tbsp red wine vinegar
Juice of half lemon
2 heaped tbsp caster sugar
40g (1½ oz) butter
Salt, pepper

A sweet and sour vegetable much loved in Austria and Germany. Serve with any of the fattier meats and poultry. It goes particularly well with duck.

Peel, core and quarter the apple. Halve the cabbage and remove the thick stem.

Use the grating disc: Process the apple and cabbage together.

Put into a large bowl with the vinegar and lemon juice. Stir in the sugar and add the butter, cut into 4 or 5 lumps. Cover partially with cling film and MICROWAVE ON HIGH for 15 minutes, stirring two or three times through the gap. Cover tightly and leave to stand for 15 minutes before serving. Season with salt and pepper if desired.

Artichoke Casserole

APPROX TIME 21 MINUTES

Serves 3 to 4

150ml (¼ pt) water
1 vegetable or beef stock cube
1 tbsp soy sauce
Salt, pepper
450g (1 lb) Jerusalem artichokes
4 young leeks, washed & trimmed
2 small potatoes, peeled
1 tomato
1 celery stalk
½ red pepper
1 level tbsp cornflour
1 x 110ml (4 fl oz) bottle Tomato Juice Cocktail

Without the Magimix this dish would be laborious to prepare and the artichokes would blacken before all were sliced. Serve the casserole as a vegetable or vegetarian supper dish.

Put the water in a jug and MICROWAVE ON HIGH for 1¾ minutes or until boiling. Stir in the stock cube, soy sauce and salt and pepper to taste.

Use the slicing disc: Peel and process the artichokes, then slice in the remaining vegetables.

Mix the vegetables thoroughly in a large shallow dish making sure to separate the artichoke slices. Add the stock, cover loosely with cling film and MICROWAVE ON HIGH for 5 minutes.

Blend the cornflour with the tomato cocktail and stir into the vegetables. Cover and MICROWAVE ON HIGH for 10 to 15 minutes or until the artichokes are tender.

Chip Fries

APPROX TIME 5 MINUTES

Serves 3

300g (¾ lb) potatoes
1 tbsp vegetable oil
Salt

You can make as large a quantity as you like increasing the Microwave time accordingly and stirring several times. 1½ lb potatoes will take 5½ to 6 minutes and they should be cooked in a large shallow dish.

Use the French Fry Potato Disc: Peel and cut the potatoes to a size that will just fit the tube. Process into chips.

Pat dry on kitchen paper.

Put into a dish and mix in the oil so that the chips are completely coated.

MICROWAVE ON HIGH for 3 to 3½ minutes, stirring once or twice until the chips soften slightly. Sprinkle with salt and brown under the grill.

If the cooking dish is unsuitable transfer to a flameproof plate to brown.

Cauliflower Purée

Use frozen or fresh cauliflower florettes in this recipe which has a pleasantly rough texture.

Put the cauliflower into a large mixing bowl or deep dish, adding 4 tablespoons water if using fresh cauliflower. Cover and MICROWAVE ON HIGH for 5 minutes.

Use the double-bladed knife: Process the cauliflower until finely chopped. It may be necessary to do this in two batches. Return to the mixing bowl.

Without rinsing put ¼ pint of the milk into the Magimix bowl and add the flour, margarine, garlic and bay leaf powder while the motor is running.

Stir the mixture into the cauliflower with the remaining milk and season to taste with salt and pepper. Partially cover with cling film and MICROWAVE ON HIGH for 10 to 12 minutes, beating occasionally with a whisk through the gap.

Serve from the dish or pour into a smaller dish and sprinkle with the crumbs.

APPROX TIME 16 MINUTES

Serves 6

450g (1 lb) frozen cauliflower florettes *or*
300g (¾ lb) fresh cauliflower florettes

600ml (1 pt) milk

25g (1 oz) flour

25g (1 oz) soft margarine

1 clove garlic, peeled

¼ tsp bay leaf powder

Salt, pepper

1 rounded tbsp toasted breadcrumbs (prepared with the double-bladed knife)

Pasta Bows in Tomato Sauce

APPROX TIME 10 MINUTES
Pasta serves 4
Sauce makes 500ml (1 pt)
225g (8 oz) pasta bows or shells
1 tsp vegetable oil
¼ onion
½ clove garlic
1 rounded tbsp flour
396g (14 oz) can tomatoes
1 tsp dried basil
2 tbsp tomato purée
25g (1 oz) butter
1 beef stock cube, crumbled
Salt, pepper
3 tbsp medium red wine
Grated Parmesan cheese

This is a quick as a flash sauce which you could use with fish, meat or vegetables equally well.

First cook the pasta – two-thirds fill a 1¼l (3 pt) casserole with boiling salted water and stir in the oil. Add the pasta and without covering, MICROWAVE ON HIGH for 6 minutes. Cover and leave while preparing the sauce. The pasta will continue cooking during this time.

Use the double-bladed knife: Chop the onion and garlic, then add the flour, contents of the tomato can, basil, tomato purée and the butter added in small pieces. Process until well blended.

Put into a large bowl, add the stock cube, season with salt and pepper and MICROWAVE ON HIGH for 4 to 5 minutes, whisking thoroughly after each minute. Stir in the wine.

Drain the pasta, put back into the casserole and pour half the sauce over. Sprinkle with grated Parmesan cheese.

Freeze the remaining sauce for use on another occasion.

Vichy Carrots

APPROX TIME 14 MINUTES
Serves 4
450g (1 lb) carrots
Hot water
Salt
15g (½ oz) butter
¼ tsp sugar
Few sprigs fresh parsley

Slice the carrots or for a change process them using the chipper disc. For the latter method you will need to use carrots which are at least 4cm (1½") in diameter. Whichever way you choose to process the carrots keep them as upright as possible to ensure an even shape.

Use the slicing disc: Prepare the carrots and process finely.

Put into an oval casserole. Add water to come about half-way up the carrots and stir in the salt (do not sprinkle on the top). Add the butter and sugar. Cover with a lid or very loosely with cling film and MICROWAVE ON HIGH for 10 to 12 minutes, stirring occasionally. Leave to stand for 3 or 4 minutes before draining, depending on how tender you wish to have your carrots.

Use the double-bladed knife: Chop the parsley finely. Sprinkle over the carrots just before serving.

Preserves and Confectionery

Chocolate Orange Pyramids

APPROX TIME 7 MINUTES

Makes 10 to 16 pyramids
Peel of 3 small Jaffa oranges
6 tbsp water
2 rounded tbsp granulated sugar
75g (3 oz) plain flavoured cooking chocolate

Chocolate addicts who can't resist buying expensive chocolate covered crystallised orange peel will be able to enjoy lots of these at a very economical cost. Don't throw away the peel next time you eat an orange – use it up this way.

Quarter the oranges and remove the peel. On a flat surface shave away most but not all of the thick white pith.

Use the thin slicing disc: Place the pieces of peel so that they are tightly packed and upright in the feed tube. Process the orange peel into fine thin strips. Put the water in a large glass measuring jug and add the peel. MICROWAVE ON HIGH for 3 minutes. Stir in the sugar until it is dissolved. MICROWAVE ON HIGH for 2 minutes. Add the chocolate broken in pieces and MICROWAVE ON HIGH for 1 ½ to 2 minutes until the mixture is boiling. Spoon small pyramids of the mixture into sweet paper cases and refrigerate or leave until quite cold and set.

Rhubarb and Apple Conserve

APPROX TIME 20 MINUTES

Makes 2 jars
350g (12 oz) rhubarb, weighed after trimming
1 x 225g (8 oz) cooking apple
1 tbsp fresh lemon juice
1 rounded tsp ground ginger
450 g (1 lb) granulated sugar

The rosy glow gives this conserve instant 'eye appeal' and the flavour is as fresh as you would expect.

Use the double-bladed knife: Process the rhubarb roughly, breaking the stems as you add them. Quarter the apples and core but do not peel. Cut up and process with the rhubarb until all the apple is finely chopped. Add the lemon juice and ginger.

Transfer to a very large heat resistant bowl. Cover partially with cling film and MICROWAVE ON HIGH for 5 minutes until pulped. Stir in the sugar. Cover with greaseproof paper and MICROWAVE ON HIGH for 12 to 15 minutes or until a spoonful placed on a chilled saucer wrinkles.

Pour into sterilized hot jars and cover with jam pot covers or cling film.

To sterilize the jars put a little water in each and microwave until boiling. Use oven gloves when preparing the jam.

Clear Citrus Marmalade

APPROX TIME 33 MINUTES
Makes 3 x 1 lb jars
1 grapefruit
1 orange
1 lemon
1kg (2 lb) preserving or granulated sugar
Small knob of butter

Marmalade made in the microwave oven has a thick syrupy texture and an exceptionally clear colour and retains all the citrus flavour.

Wash and dry the fruit. Cut into quarters. Pare away the outside peel thinly and set aside.

Use the double-bladed knife: Chop the fruit finely (this includes the pith, flesh and pips).

Put into a large heatproof bowl with 450ml (¾ pt) boiling water. MICROWAVE ON HIGH for 10 minutes.

Use the slicing disc: Process the reserved peel finely.

Press the cooked pulp through a sieve into another large bowl so that all the juice is squeezed out. Stir in the peel and MICROWAVE ON HIGH for 10 minutes or until the peel is tender but not soft, stirring once during cooking.

Stir in the sugar thoroughly. The heat of the juice should help it to dissolve more quickly. MICROWAVE ON HIGH for 10 minutes or until a spoonful of syrup wrinkles when put on a cold plate. Stir in the butter half way through cooking to prevent the syrup from foaming.

Pot in hot sterilized jars and seal with jam pot covers or cover with cling film.

For longer term storage fill the jars to within 1" of the rim, cover loosely with cling film and return to the microwave oven briefly until the film balloons. Remove the jars carefully with oven gloves.

Apple, Date and Walnut Chutney

APPROX TIME 16 MINUTES
Makes 2 jars
450g (1 lb) cooking apples
100g (4 oz) carrots, scraped
100g (4 oz, ½ pkt) dates
50g (2 oz) walnuts
50g (2 oz) raisins
3 tbsp fresh lemon juice
225g (8 oz) muscavado sugar
1 heaped tsp salt
150ml (¼ pint) red wine *or*
120ml (4 fl oz) cider vinegar and
1 tbsp tomato purée

This is a sweet chutney which could almost be described as a quick mincemeat but it can be converted to a ploughman's pickle in an instant. Substitute cider vinegar for the wine and add a tablespoon of tomato purée. You could make one sweet and one savoury jar by dividing the ingredients before adding the wine and cooking simultaneously in two smaller bowls. Muscavado sugar gives the best flavour but if you are unable to purchase this substitute dark brown sugar.

Quarter and core the apples.

Use the double-bladed knife: Chop the apples, carrots, dates and nuts.

Put into a large bowl and stir in the raisins, lemon juice, sugar, salt and wine (or vinegar and tomato purée).

MICROWAVE ON HIGH for 15 to 16 minutes, stirring occasionally until the mixture begins to thicken.

Pot the chutney in sterilized jars, filling to an inch below the rim. Cover the tops loosely with cling film and MICROWAVE ON HIGH for 15 to 20 seconds to tighten the film and form a seal. The chutney improves with keeping.

Barrelos

APPROX TIME 7 MINUTES
+ CHILLING TIME
Makes 40 pieces
100g (4 oz) sifted icing sugar
100g (4 oz) ground almonds
½ beaten egg
½ tsp orange flower water
3 tbsp double cream
15g (½ oz) butter
1 tbsp water
100g (4 oz) plain flavoured cooking chocolate
Cornflour

An almond paste confection stuffed with truffle.

Use the plastic blade: Combine the icing sugar, ground almonds, egg and orange flower water until a smooth paste is formed. Do not overwork or the almonds will become oily. Divide into 4 pieces and form into sausage shapes. Roll each to an oblong 5cm (2") wide. Trim the edges.

Put the cream in a medium bowl and MICROWAVE ON HIGH for ½ to 1 minute until boiling. Stir in the butter and 1 tbsp water. MICROWAVE ON HIGH for 1 minute. Add the chocolate broken into pieces and MICROWAVE ON HIGH for 2 minutes or until melted. Chill for ½ hour or until the mixture begins to thicken. Return to the Magimix and process until the consistency is that of a malleable paste.

Divide the chocolate mixture into 4 equal pieces and roll between hands

dipped in cornflour (so that the mixture will not stick) to a rope the length of the almond paste.

Place in the centre of the almond paste and roll up the long sides to enclose the filling. Chill until firm, then cut into 1cm (⅜") slices. Put into sweet paper cases and store in the refrigerator.

Praline

APPROX TIME 8 MINUTES

Makes 175g (6 oz)

50g (2 oz) shelled unskinned whole almonds

100g (4 oz) granulated sugar

Praline is easy to make using the Magimix and the Microwave oven. There are no sticky pans to wash up and the mixture can be processed as finely as you wish, enabling it to be used as toppings for ice cream, desserts or in cake mixtures. Make a double quantity and store in a plastic box to use as required, allowing a few minutes more cooking time. The mixture becomes very hot during cooking, so use oven gloves to protect your hands.

Mix the almonds and sugar on a double sheet of non-stick paper that just fits the oven shelf.

MICROWAVE ON HIGH for 5 to 8 minutes, stirring frequently with a wooden spoon until all the sugar is melted and a brown syrup forms. Leave until hard. (It is dangerous to overcook the mixture as it could burn).

Use the double-bladed knife: Break up the almond brittle and process until pulverized.

Cakes, Puddings and Desserts

Praline and Orange Crown

APPROX TIME 7 MINUTES
Serves 8
100g (4 oz) butter
100g (4 oz) caster sugar
1 level tsp baking powder
¼ tsp vanilla essence
1 tbsp fresh orange juice
Few drops orange food colouring
2 large eggs
100g (4 oz) sifted plain flower
4 rounded tbsp praline

Use a microwave proof savarin ring or make your own by placing a narrow diametered straight-sided glass or jar into the centre of a mixing bowl.

Put the butter on a small plate and MICROWAVE ON HIGH for 15 to 20 seconds to soften.

Use the double-bladed knife: Put the butter and sugar in the Magimix bowl and process until light and fluffy. While the motor is still running add the baking powder, vanilla essence, orange juice, colouring and the eggs one at a time. Remove the Magimix lid, add half the flour, then replace the lid and switch on and off quickly. Repeat with the remaining flour. Put half the mixture into a suitable greased savarin ring. Add most of the praline (see recipe, page 27), to the remaining cake mix and switch on and off briefly to mix. Put on the top of the plain mixture and swirl through with a spoon handle.

MICROWAVE ON HIGH for 4 minutes or until just dry on top. leave for a few minutes before turning out and sprinkle the remaining praline on top.

Apple Clafoutis

APPROX TIME 10 MINUTES
Serves 5 to 6
450g (1 lb) cooking apples
2 large eggs
100g (4 oz) caster sugar
½ teaspoon vanilla essence
50g (2 oz) sifted self-raising flour

Eat this family dessert hot or cold. It greatly improves after a day's rest in the refrigerator.

Peel, quarter and core the apples.

Use the slicing disc: Slice the apples coarsely. Transfer to a large shallow flame-proof dish. Remove the slicing disc and wipe out the Magimix bowl.

Use the plastic blade: Beat the eggs until fluffy. Add the sugar and vanilla essence while the motor is running, beating until the mixture thickens. Add the flour in three parts, removing the lid each time so that the flour can be evenly distributed when processed. After each addition switch the motor quickly on and off so that the flour is folded in.

Pour the sponge mixture evenly over the apples (there is no need to add extra sugar as the topping is sweet). MICROWAVE ON HIGH for 6 to 8 minutes, turning the dish occasionally until the mixture is just dry on top.

Brown under the grill.

Peach Treacle Upside-Down Cake

APPROX TIME 7 MINUTES

Serves 6

1 tbsp black treacle
410 g (14½ oz) can sliced peaches
1 large egg
1 rounded tbsp soft brown sugar
50g (2 oz) soft margarine
75g (3 oz) sifted plain flour
1 rounded tsp baking powder
1 rounded tbsp ground almonds
1 tbsp water

Use soft dark brown sugar for better texture, flavour and colour in this cake which can also be eaten hot. But you must resist eating it immediately it is cooked or the syrup will burn your mouth.

Grease a shallow 24cm (9") dish. Put in the treacle and MICROWAVE ON HIGH for 5 seconds, then swirl over the base. Drain the peaches and arrange the slices decoratively in the base of the dish, bearing in mind that the pattern will show when the cake is turned out.

Use the double-bladed knife: Add the remaining ingredients and process for about 30 seconds or until mixed.

Place the mixture in teaspoonsful over the peaches. It may not be necessary to spread it very much as this occurs during cooking.

MICROWAVE ON HIGH for 5 to 6 minutes, turning if necessary until the mixture is just dry on top.

Remove with oven gloves and leave for a few minutes before turning out.

Carrot and Marmalade Sponge Pudding

APPROX TIME 7 MINUTES

Serves 6

3 tbsp marmalade
175g (6 oz) carrots
100g (4 oz) soft butter or margarine
100g (4 oz) caster sugar
2 large eggs
100g (4 oz) sifted self-raising flour

This is a most delicious pudding suitable for family meals or for entertaining. It is surprising how many dinner guests prefer a nice home-made pud to cold 'trolley' type desserts.

Grease a 1·2-1·5 L (2-2½ pt) pudding basin and spoon the marmalade into the base.

MICROWAVE ON HIGH for 10 seconds to soften and spread the marmalade.

Use the grating disc: Grate the peeled carrots, remove from the processor and set aside.

Use the plastic blade: Put the butter (or margarine) and sugar in the Magimix bowl and process until light and fluffy (about 20 seconds). Add the egg followed by the carrot while the motor is still running. Add the flour in two lots quickly switching on and off after each addition.

Put the mixture in the prepared pudding basin and without covering, MICROWAVE ON HIGH for 5 to 6 minutes, turning if necessary until the centre top is only just dry.

Leave for a few minutes before turning on to a serving dish.

Spicy Bran Ring

APPROX TIME 7½ MINUTES

Serves 8 to 10

150g (5 oz) soft margarine
100g (4 oz) soft light brown sugar
2 tbsp golden syrup
2 tbsp milk
25g (1 oz) walnuts
1 level tsp ground ginger
2 large eggs
15 glacé cherries
75g (3 oz) self-raising flour
1 level tsp baking powder
75g (3 oz) bran
75g (3 oz) sifted icing sugar
1 tbsp clear honey
2 tbsp warm water
Glacé cherries
Walnut halves

An attractive wholesome cake that is both appetising and healthy since it comes into the 'high fibre' category. To avoid spilling, when microwaving cake mixtures, only two-thirds fill the dish.

Grease a plastic, porcelain or glass savarin ring mould.

Use the double-bladed knife: Process the margarine, sugar, syrup, milk, ginger and walnuts thoroughly. Feed in the eggs and cherries. Lastly add the flour, baking powder and bran, and process briefly in 2 or 3 short bursts. The Magimix bowl will be full but as the batter is sticky it will not seep out.

Smooth the mixture into the prepared dish and MICROWAVE ON HIGH for 5½ to 6 minutes until barely dry on top. Turn the dish 90° three times during cooking if necessary.

Leave in the dish for a few moments before turning out on to a serving plate. Use oven gloves for this.

Use the plastic blade: Combine the icing sugar, honey and water and process until smooth. This icing is fairly thin. Spoon over the hot cake to form a brittle see-through icing.

Decorate with glacé cherries and nuts.

Flowerpot Cake

APPROX TIME 10 MINUTES
Serves 6
100g (4 oz) butter
100g (4 oz) sugar
2 eggs (size 3), beaten
100g (4 oz) self-raising flour
50g (2 oz) cocoa powder
50g (2 oz) ground almonds
2 tbsp honey
3 to 4 tbsp milk
100g (4 oz) block marzipan
Red food colouring
Green food colouring
Edible sugar flowers
1 clay flower pot

This pretty chocolate cake will have all your teatime guests begging for the recipe. Do not use plastic cling film to line the flowerpot since the cake needs a rough, rather than a smooth, finish.

Use the plastic blade: Cream the butter and sugar together until light and fluffy. Add the remaining cake ingredients and sufficient milk to form a soft mixture. Be careful not to overprocess.

Line the base of a new flower pot 15cm (6") in diameter and height with a disc of non-stick paper. Grease the sides throroughly. Half fill with the cake mixture and MICROWAVE ON HIGH for 5 to 6 minutes until just dry on top. Turn out carefully on to a wire cooling rack.

When the cake is cold reverse it on to a large piece of plastic cling film. Remove a thin slice from the top of the cake so that the top is not shiny and replace in the flowerpot, folding the edges of the plastic film over the sides so that the cake can be lifted out for serving.

Colour three-quarters of the marzipan green and form into branches and leaves and make small red berries with the remainder. Fix the branches on to the cake using cocktail sticks and decorate with the berries and flowers.